LIFE'S
POETIC
GLOSSARY

LIFE'S POETIC GLOSSARY

THE HUMANITY OF EVERYDAY WORDS

KRISTA KUJAT

Published by A Poetic Life

ISBN: 979-8-3410804-6-1 (Paperback)

Edited by Alexa Johansen, Ph.D.

Cover design by Maxobiz.

Graphics by Zeno Zokalj.

Formatting by David Provolo.

First printing edition 2024.

A Poetic Life
28159 N 96th Place
Scottsdale, AZ 85262

info@kristakujat.com

PRAISE FOR *LIFE'S POETIC GLOSSARY*

In this exquisite glossary of words, Kujat masterfully balances simplicity with depth. She crafts poems that are both accessible and profoundly moving. Each piece is a testament to her ability to distill complex emotions into clear, resonant language, adorned with beautiful imagery that lingers long after the final line. Kujat invites readers to explore the world through a lens that is both fresh and familiar, making this collection a must-read for anyone who appreciates the power of well-crafted verse.

Derrick Engoy
Poet, Writer, Pastor

A timeless work of art and literary creativity. I could read this collection of poetry again and again with each new morning and evening—and *still* never run out of depth and beauty to discover! Kujat's definitions have made my jaw drop with awe, my mouth spread into a delighted smile, my voice sing out in laughter, and my eyes widen from feeling so suddenly and deeply moved. As a poet and artist, I can attest to becoming a more beautiful version of myself after simply having experienced Kujat's heart and perspective in the form of words. Kujat has offered us poetry that not only inspires, but nurtures, soothes, and dares.

Alexa Johansen, Ph.D.
Founder and CEO of GoldScriptCo
Author of *Dear Girl*

Pouring over Kujat's glossary unraveled me. In a time of constant, instant gratification and incessant death by scrolling, Kujat's rare, delicately devastating, utterly beautiful *Life's Poetic Glossary* is a raging, yet quiet defiance. It is a revelation revolution. An unveiling of how we can choose to become the prisoners or liberators of the meaning-making that makes or breaks us. Her meditations allow us to savor the gift of each passing moment. Kujat's words pour pure freedom into us in a way that awakens us. As you read through these pages, you, too, will become inspired to give yourself the permission to breathe in your own life, in your own time, on your own terms, in your own words.

Kashmir Birk
CEO of The True North

Life's Poetic Glossary is a treasure trove of perceptive metaphors for some of the most important experiences we encounter in life. Kujat's descriptions take your breath away, inviting you to touch each word at the depth of its essence, beckoning forth what is longing to happen. Kujat gives birth to a dictionary that will be quoted and spoken for decades to come. This is a guide to emotional and spiritual wisdom, with words that will resonate well past reading them. It is a gift that will be passed on and on.

Elizabeth Husserl
Author of *The Power of Enough*
Co-Founder of Peak360 Wealth Management

A masterpiece! In this collection, poetry jams with honest self-inquiry to reveal and reclaim one's own lexicon. Picking this book up is a choice to jump heart-first into your own experience of discovery—a discovery where new definitions of many everyday words (along with a few lesser-known words) pull, pry, and provoke you toward a greater definition of self and lived experiences. Kujat masterfully evokes a full-bodied, sensory experience that leaves you to quietly ponder, "What is my own life glossary?" I was moved, inspired, and changed—a feat only possible in the presence of a wise soul following the pounding of her own heart.

Pick up this book and watch yourself breathe more deeply as you sink further into your chair, into your soul, and into your beautifully-layered life.

Cindy Kennedy
Creator of The Center for Sass'n Soul

I desire this rich and thoughtful book on my nightstand to help me start and end my day with its wise insights and soothing wisdom. These thought- and heart-provoking words for modern life will cause you to pause, reflect, and be with the energetics of each word. Greater self-awareness, joy, delight, groundedness, and play await as you dive deeply into Kujat's wisdom and access your own. I will read this collection again and again.

Kim Shirley
Creator of Reclaim Your Wild

Enchanting, powerful, and magical. Self-growth, or dare I say self-development, had a love affair with poetry. You'll be wistful and wiser with every page. It is a wonder to read a book of poetry that feels mystical while offering goddess-like wisdom in ways I haven't read before. It's infused with intelligence. Kujat brings all my senses to alertness as she offers slices of her life, lived boldly with missteps, deep reflections, and the kind of knowledge only gained in living wild and free amidst systems not built for the wild and free. She takes everyday words and threads together stories, meaning, and love with ease.

Sara Alvarado
Author of *Dreaming in Spanish: A Memoir*

This collection is dedicated to the two people
who gave me the gift of being human:
Mom & Dad

Infinite thanks to my closest friends and partners
who've taught me more about being myself
than any curriculum ever could.

Contents

Prologue

In high school, a best friend alerted me to the fact that I had a condition called *malapropism*. When I opened the dictionary, I learned malapropism is "the act or habit of misusing words ridiculously, especially by the confusion of words that are similar in sound." This can be either hilarious or humiliating, depending on which lens I'm looking at the situation through.

For example, in tenth grade biology class, when examining an octopus's tentacles, I referred to the tentacles as "testicles." My lab group laughed. My cheeks flushed hot pink. I laughed to save face.

As someone who doubted whether the words that came out of my mouth were accurate or not, I eventually found that the poetry of words, spoken in images, was far more precise than any dictionary definition could garner for being "right" or "wrong."

As for my malapropism condition, I like to think most of the words that come out of my mouth "inaccurately" aren't as inaccurate as they sound. After all, my teenage hormones (paired with monstrous shyness) were simply navigating the steamy presence of my lab partner;

I'd be remiss if I failed to admit that testicles were indeed on my mind. Perhaps malapropism could be more aptly explained as two words that are *both* appropriate, depending on whose mind you're inside of. But, I digress.

Unlike Sanskrit, which has ninety-six words for *love*, and Persian, which has eighty words, English only has one.

A French love interest once told me "je t'aime" should exclusively be used for the person you are close to and love dearly. He found it both confusing and offensive to hear me say things like "I love chocolate cake" when I used the same word to describe my feelings for him. It's not lost on me that language has limits; there are subtleties of meaning that often go unacknowledged or unspoken.

Language barriers and vernacular syndromes aside, I believe there is a much richer vocabulary on the horizon that is just waiting for us to engage with and discover—a language that is better suited for the era we are living in; one that reaches beyond dictionary definitions rooted in mindsets of the status quo established thousands of years ago.

Writing this glossary became a homage to celebrate the rarely-acknowledged nuances of meaning held in the heart, while thumping along the unbridled ride of being human.

You might think of each reimagined definition in this book like an ode to the lived experience of these words. As you read each poem, consider how your relationship to words informs how you relate to your sense of self, while fumbling toward deeper fulfillment.

For myself, being steeped in this study of unspoken subtleties unlocked a freedom from the limits of language that carry age-old associations and overused generalizations. Ultimately, I was left with a peace that enveloped my own experience of being human.

Welcome to an odyssey of reimagining everyday words as a sacred lexicon— perhaps encompassing all you could possibly feel, but never before had the words for.

awe is

: a catalyst for imagining the unimaginable

Awe likes to be naked while riding wild horses bareback in the rain.

Awe collapses all carefully-constructed realities by galloping outside the guardrails of rules, successes of the past, and any agreements that have ever been made by anyone, anywhere, anytime.

Awe rides forces of nature to create something beyond what could have existed without their fusion.

Awe's untamed muscles rippling over open fields will make you wonder not *whether* a miracle will happen, but when.

beauty is

: a rose, deeply layered and unabashedly captivating

: a flaming sunset flanked by the tenderness of ballet
pinks and lounging lavenders, affirming that passion
and compassion live in the same sky

: a permeating warmth that floods the sternum, seeps
through the ribcage, and drips into every cell with
a reminder that connection is within arm's reach

: a state of being that requires no armor

What I know about beauty is that, in its most relentless
form, it's identity-shattering.

becoming is

: the pathway toward
your insides converging
with the outside world

: defining and refining
the altar of self-expression
as the anthem for
loving oneself
plays on

: feeling limp and impotent
resting and reckoning
with all the life lived so far
and daring to ask
what's waiting to be
birthed
into the
beyond?

betrayal is

: something beautiful upheld with a lie

: a doorway to sublime sobriety while reckoning
with rude realities

What I know about betrayal is that it's a window to see which dreams were too small and which expectations were too low.

What I know about betrayal is that its architecture is built upon a thousand flimsy permission slips that read "use me as you see fit," while denying a deeper foundation of needs and desires.

What I know about betrayal is that, right there, in the gap between what you *want* to believe and what you know to be true, is where you become liberated from false hope and empowered with radical honesty.

What I know about betrayal is that, once you see the lies you believed, you are ushered into a new corridor that leads to one destination: your power.

the beyond is

: a touchless caress
coaxing you to be loved
beyond the flesh of
understanding

: savoring such
exquisite intimacy
with the intangible
that you forget yourself
and remember
yourself anew

a blessing is

: benevolence that rekindles faith in possibilities

: a stranger's compassion that cracks open self-forgiveness

: a bowl full of insights when you're ready
to harvest the fruits of your labor

: laborless love ushering you along your path,
exactly as you are

bliss is

: an unhurried morning under the gentle weight
of forgiving sheets

: time-traveling through the wordless warmth of a gaze

: molten chocolate playing an undying symphony
from tongue to toes

: communing with the timeless blaze of the sun and
the ageless heart of the horizon

What I know about bliss is that, when you reach for it, it
disappears—just like a word you're trying to remember,
one that skips across the ridgeline of your tongue as you try
to chase it down.

What I know about bliss is that it makes urgency disappear,
loneliness extinct, and gratitude explode.

What I know about bliss is that no human is excluded from
its visceral music.

a calling is

: an invisible cord wrapped
around your chest,
tethered to the stars,
pulling you toward your
destiny to shine

: an ecstatic magnetism between
the freedom of formlessness
and the fulfillment of form

courage is

: the triumph of being yourself

desire is

: fueled by the longing to be, to belong, and to become

: an undeniable reality waiting to be galvanized and actualized

What I know about desire is that it's deeper than a craving, more consistent than a whim, more assured than a want, and more empowered than a need.

More about desire...

Desire's voice sounds like fire crackling on a rainy day. When she speaks, she burns the barriers that naysayers once built up like dams.

The grandmother of Desire, De Sidere, came from the stars. Rumors have it that De Sidere was named in an effort to offer a word for when we look at a starless night sky and ardently feel an absence—a longing. After all, the stars usher in the magic and completeness of the night.

discernment is

: an inner filter that knows whether a slice of
chocolate cake or a handsome date is an
empty craving or a need for nourishment

: decoding façades from authenticity

: understanding the difference between walls
and boundaries

: knowing when to step back from fixing the unfixable,
changing the unchangeable, or tossing the loss

: detecting when perfection is driven by protection
or devotion

What I know about discernment is that every moment is as
unique as the last and, despite the impulse to reach for tools
that have worked in the past, sometimes what's needed is
space and time for confusion to reveal its many facets.

More about discernment...

Discernment's sophisticated pixie cut leaves nothing to hide
behind, which is fitting for her long-standing position as
Lead Assessment Officer at the Office of Transparency.

The Office of Transparency is a high order of the Court of Personal Truths—far higher than that of the Supreme Court, which is strictly governed by judgments of rights and wrongs. Unlike Judgment, Discernment makes decisions based on honoring her integrity, self-fulfillment, and self-empowerment, leaving no room for "unfairness" in the court's jargon. Discernment is most known for her widely celebrated court case: Integrity vs Self-Sacrifice.

What others covet most about Discernment is that she makes decisions without projecting disappointments from the past onto the future, while taking wisdom from the past to make favorable choices for the present. Her keen sense for not throwing the baby out with the bathwater is one of the many reasons why people seek out her counsel, especially after a devastating loss or heartbreak.

As you can imagine, since Discernment's livelihood hinges on clarity, her greatest fear is having a lack of it. On her days off from attending the Court of Personal Truths, Discernment lets herself be a hot mess. She goes to the beach, turns up the volume on a steamy hip-hop track blaring through her earbuds, then shimmies her hips as the waves crash against her calves. Discernment knows that when she lets the whole gamut of murky emotions wriggle through her body, clarity emerges.

divine is

: an elevated knowing, unbound by the density of flesh
and bones, untethered to the heart's imprints or
the body's narratives

The Divine is a cohort of invisible operators behind the
scenes who chaperone us toward expansion. They drink air
for breakfast and savor sunbeams for lunch. They're futurists
of the highest calling who show you pictures of possibilities
through the language of light.

You may feel these invisible operators running shivers down
your spine. You'll know what their voices feel like when your
heart unfolds its infinite petals at high speed in a timeless
time-lapse.

duty is

: being reliable to others at the expense of being reliable
to yourself

: like thick Spanish tile, robust, sturdy, earthy—it has been tried
and tested for years; however, its uncrackable history leaves you
with an inherited foundation that is not your chosen dwelling

: a corset with chords of obligation pulled so tightly around
your ribs you don't even know your true body shape anymore

: performed under the banner of love, loyalty, and care;
yet, the banner can fall upon you like a blindfold that
keeps your desires in the dark

Duty has broad shoulders, a robust, thick torso, and wears twill,
knee-length skirts with long-sleeve cardigans. When Duty enters
a room, she moves like a large ship berthing into a harbor, slow
and steady.

Duty's 10,000-year-old birthday is coming up, but she's not keen
on celebrating. Even though she's the first to bring a gift to anyone
else's birthday party, she's simply too tired to think about her own.

Ever since Duty was a child, her greatest fear has been not knowing who she is without all the things she does. Nearly every day, Guilt comes to visit Duty for morning coffee as she writes out her to-do list. While Duty can't stand how Guilt rambles on and on with endless monologues about what she should do and why, Duty listens anyway because she believes Guilt must have the answers.

Duty's second worst fear is being called selfish.

Luckily for Duty, her neighbor, Self-Love, demonstrates that she won't die if she doesn't do all that's expected of her. In fact, she might just find herself having the time of her life while whirling around on the teacup ride at Disneyland instead of yanking out weeds in her backyard.

What Duty is so close to discovering is that it's easier than she thinks to save herself from the waterlogged weight of a thousand inherited agreements that she never chose for herself in the first place. All she needs to do is say, "Nope. No. No can do." No explanations needed.

enchantment is

: a seductive garden path attended by giggling marigold,
flirtatious fuchsia, and magnanimous magenta

: the outspoken majesty of mountains bellowing with silence

: a golden moon's hypnotic luminosity that beckons on
a night full of question marks

: a permanent twilight free from the convictions of the night
and ambitions of the day

: a captivating blend of the known and unknown, the real
and surreal, the natural and supernatural

: intoxicating scents of enraptured cardamom, blazing
turmeric, and unapologetic saffron—all awaiting the
alchemy of their destiny

: a portal to heartwarming mysteries that defy both science
and words

eros is

: a primal instinct to thrive in aliveness

: love funneled into the body's creative articulation

Eros eats fire, drinks oceans, moves mountains, and transmutes light—all while being governed by gravity.

essence is

: the you that's consistent, no matter your fingerprints, imprints, or blueprints

: a kaleidoscope of colors ready to speak rainbows, dance flames, sculpt light, and taste music

What I know about essence is that you feel it most when you're not doing or thinking anything at all.

Example of *essence* used in a sentence:

Sometimes I think self-expression would be easier if someone could just poke a needle into me, extract my *essence*, funnel it into a bottle, and enjoy it forever. The label on the bottle would read: Drink Me.

exalted is

What I know about being exalted is it happens when all the best parts of yourself are nourished by precise conditions of time, place, and circumstances. The result: an effortless, full-bodied burst into bloom.

expression is

: unleashing an illogical feeling with a wordless howl

: a channel that disempowers fear from running rampant
with ruminations

: choosing the headline of your heart when translating
your inner knowing for the outer world

: choreographing your imagination into an etch, a sketch,
a sculpture, or a word

: liberation from the untold stories in your DNA

: your legacy

What I know about expression is that it's like a garden hose;
with a gentle flow it nourishes the most delicate seedlings,
and with explosive pressure it crushes even the most robust
blooms.

What I know about expression is there's no guarantee that
you will be understood by others; but, what matters is you
understand yourself and express what matters to you.

forgiveness is

: the grace of two hearts to start over, whether together
or apart

: seeing an untold innocence tucked within someone
who has inflicted harm

: acknowledging the pain you've caused yourself or others,
then choosing to mend the misstep and stitch the lessons
into your heart

: to offer yourself compassion for not being able to see then
what you can see now

: releasing the grip on the fistful of pains that holds
your heart hostage and unfurling your fingers to receive
another's touch

: a flood of love that reaches every parched crevice
of your heart with surrendered solace

Forgiveness is a quiet cloud that floats in the air like a
possibility. She will land upon your lap when the storm of
your circumstances settle. Due to her lightness, you will only
become aware of her presence when you stop wishing the
storm never happened in the first place.

Forgiveness will often sit with you for days. The cushioned contours of her form will wrap around the shoulder of your regrets, filling you with a softened remembrance that, no matter what, you are loved.

Most come to understand that Forgiveness can't be rushed. When enough time has passed, Forgiveness will enter the living room of your heart bearing sheepskin rugs, fluffy duvets, and mattress warmers because she knows that plush, warm comforts help to usher you into surrender.

friendship is

: an invitation to be unzipped, zany, and zealous

: the fusion of boundless curiosities and bountiful discoveries

: an infinite basin for which no confession is too shallow
or too deep

: the hand that softens and shapes the clay of your heart

: the purity of presence when a friend sheds tears through
the terrain only they can travel

: like an accordion, its music can be played whether stretched
out with distance or hugged together in closeness

On Monday, Friendship's internet cut out in the middle of
filing her taxes, just before the deadline. Exasperated,
Friendship burst into tears.

Friendship considered calling her friend, SoundingBoard,
who would simply listen without prescribing opinions or
conclusions, allowing Friendship to unpack why she was so
late filing her taxes in the first place. Then, she considered
calling BossLady, who would pull her out the door to go
dancing, insisting she leave all the sulking behind. In
the end, Friendship decided to call MadHatter. When he

arrived, Madhatter didn't miss a beat in reenacting the day's melodrama as a full-fledged comedy sketch. He acted out each phone representative who robotically read their script and volleyed her from one manager to the next. By the end, Friendship and Madhatter howled with rapturous ridicule as a new inside joke was born—one they'd revisit with delight for years to come.

to give is

: to fertilize symbiosis like a bee pollinating a wildflower

: to beam like the sun, enabling flow that is free
from transactions

: to expose the vulnerability of caring, through a gesture,
gaze, or gift

: to place a pillow under a lover's head long before they
realize they've been straining to hold their head up

: to embrace the keen spirit of filling stockings with
unexpected gifts through every season

: to speak another's language

What I know about giving is that saying *thank you* is
some-times the biggest gift you can give.

What I know about giving is that, when it costs you
your peace, joy, or integrity, giving changes its name to self-
sacrifice.

grace is

: a crisis kissed by mercy

: receptivity, trust, and benevolence

: the magnificence of disengaging from drama

: saying "oh sweetie" while watching a temper tantrum
take off like a tornado

: a gentle word that suspends all angst

: an encouraging glance in the face of a misstep

Grace wears opulent silk gowns in gray tones. She has long
legs, arms, and fingers—as though each part of her has been
extended through the corridors of time, stretched by harsh-
ness, all while exuding a stillness that is breathtaking. Her
posture is attentive and alert, like an egret wading in still
waters, speaking volumes with her silence.

People who have a lot to say often don't notice how Grace
receives their words without needing to match their cadence,
rhythm, or determination. It's not that Grace doesn't speak,
it's that she speaks through the sound of her presence—
deliberate, steady, and impeccably subtle.

gratitude is

: the currency of prosperity

: reachable and kissable

: a love letter from the terrain you've traveled to
the mountain you're climbing

: a gift-wrapped dose of encouragement from
your mistakes to your second chances

: being rinsed with relief, showered with warmth,
and bathed in appreciation

: taking inventory of your footsteps to fulfillment

What I know about gratitude is that, just like anything else,
whatever you choose to focus on grows, amplifies, and
multiplies.

guilt is

: a master social influencer

: a guidepost that reveals who you're loyal to at the cost
of being loyal to yourself

What I know about guilt is that it multiplies its narratives
when the scroll of your past regrets unravels across the floor.

What I know about guilt is that it's the language of morals,
laced with all you've ever been taught, while your soul speaks
another language entirely.

More about guilt...

Guilt wears a white, starched, button-down shirt and a
perfectly-pressed black tie. He loves everything that's black
and white and has zero tolerance for any shade of gray. He
peers down through spectacles perched on his nose while
examining his ancestral moral codes, which he collects like
treasured antiquities.

Guilt loves conducting your heartstrings to play grand reper-
toires of pathos, plagiarized from the past. His melodies swoon
and serenade you with unsolicited judgments about what you
should do, what you should say, and who you should be.

Guilt is determined to enforce past agreements as he whispers in your ear with his hot, skanky breath:

"You agreed to do this."
"You've always done that."
"Who are you to change?"

Meanwhile, Doubt is an enthusiastic backup singer to Guilt's tune. Doubt croons and coos her sultry song into your ears: "Were you too brash? Too harsh? Too severe? Unkind? Uncaring? Unclear? Unforgiving?"

Long after his song ends, Guilt still remains close, even perched on your shoulder most nights. He knows the only reason you'd ever seek his advice is rooted in the concern of doing "The Wrong Thing."

Guilt will never disclose that other people's reactions have nothing to do with your worthiness. Guilt will also never encourage you to follow your heart's desire, because as soon as you name them, he becomes disempowered.

harmony is

: two hearts with resonant voices

: void of competition

: never setting an alarm

Harmony feels relaxed when everything is in its place. And when she feels relaxed, she feels at peace.

Harmony is known to remind her friends that, sometimes, it's distance (not closeness) that will make you feel at ease.

hope is

: a balloon fueled with beautiful suggestions that keep you buoyant, offering relief from gravity

: a placeholder for your heart's desires that haven't yet come to fruition

: permission to reimagine existing conditions

: a daydream that asks nothing of you

: a filter that tints how you see the world, and sometimes prevents you from seeing things as they are

ACT I

Sometimes, Hope dresses up like an angel with wispy wings. She confidently enters stage right with a benevolent half-smile. When Hope dresses up like an angel, you may feel a flutter awaken inside of you—a sense of knowing that you've been blessed with a special kind of fate. Hope, while in the role of an angel, can help you to accept that no matter how hard challenges may be, you're deserving of beautiful outcomes.

However, Hope dressed as an angel can easily set you up for "wishful thinking." Unfortunately, in this case, Hope may fail to remind you it's important to put faith into action by taking concrete steps toward your dreams. Although the playwright gave Hope minimal lines, she sure does make you feel good when she breaks the fourth wall and winks at you.

ACT 2

Other times, Hope dresses up like a real estate agent who sells billion-dollar dream homes. The set designer has ensured every decorative piece on stage fills you with a dreamy sense of a promising future. Hope, in the role of a real estate agent, wears a white pantsuit and walks to center stage with authority, delivering meticulously scripted monologues about the custom shelving in the walk-in closet, which is big enough to be a boutique. She's particularly enthusiastic about selling you a house that has an opulent infinity pool with a sunset view. This is when the lighting designer cues a dreamy orange glow to illuminate the sunset backdrop. You know what you're seeing isn't real, but the suggestion of bliss beyond what you know becomes hypnotic.

Hope the real estate agent has a tricky side—she can make you believe that a luxurious house is precisely the thing that will make you happy. Because she's focused on what's alluring about the house, she won't emphasize the important detail that buying a hundred-year-old home comes with the territory of unforeseen repairs. At times like this, you'll realize the very things you hope for can deliver rude realities. You'll start to see where the lines between fantasy and reality intersect, and become awakened to the difference between delusion and discernment.

ACT 3

Hope may dress up as a lover who looks good on paper, wearing extensive lists on their sleeves equivalent to the length of a CVS receipt. The lists outline a tall order that includes how you want your lover to breathe in their sleep, how you want them to anticipate your needs, and that they must be game for giving the benefit of the doubt while asking questions with curiosity. Hope dances around like a twirling dervish with a pen in hand, ready to add more scribbles to the list. In this role, Hope can distract you from your true desire, which is to enjoy the company of someone who has a heart of gold.

ACT 4

Hope may dress up like a nurse, bringing scanners and stethoscopes by your bedside to give you an honest appraisal of where your heart is at. When you see Hope dressed as a nurse in her crisp, white uniform, she looks you straight in the eyes and tells you that you can get through anything. This is, by far, one of Hope's most fortuitous charms. Even if Hope is not always the one who knows what's best for you, she'll encourage you unconditionally.

ACT 5

Perhaps Hope's favorite role is when she dresses up as a Fairy Godmother. She paints her nails Big Apple Red and wears heels that look like glass slippers kissed with glitter. She carries a bag full of wit and magic wands. If you join her on stage to make-believe, you'll find your dreams actually can come true—so long as you feel them come alive in your body with all of your might.

horrible is

: a tragedy that no one deserves, but sometimes happens

: an event that requires unapologetically long hugs

humility is

: being at the mercy of miracles

: when you see a friend with new eyes—not because of how
they have changed, but because of how you have changed

: becoming sobered to the big and small ways you've engaged
in the cycle of pain and punishment

: realizing the path to self-forgiveness is the same for
a murderer or a saint

: knowing none of us are exempt from being human

What I know about humility is that it's not only a doorway
to self-compassion, it also disarms those who are privy to
witnessing it.

identity is

: a constellation of habits

: the first thought upon waking and the final thought
before drifting into slumber

: selecting which belongings to shove into a backpack
when the fire alarm goes off

: choosing the most fitting avatar to represent your insides

: having an idea of who you think you need to be in order
to be yourself

: realizing we are more shaped by the cult in the word culture
than we realize

What I know about identity is that defining ourselves in order
to be ourselves is not always necessary.

What I know about identity is that it shatters in the eye of the
storm and shreds through the eye of the needle.

What I know about identity is that when it dies, it swallows
every belief and offers a forgiving blank canvas to begin again.

innocence is

: a heart that claims wonder as its name

: deserving of the benefit of the doubt

: putting one foot in front of the other, free from stories
of stumbling

: an undying willingness to begin again

What I know about innocence is that, when you embrace it
wholeheartedly, its unfiltered lens will affirm that you are,
indeed, faultless.

intuition is

: the native language of
your heart and guts

: communion with
unbound luminosity
making the invisible visible

: the heartbeat of
your inner eyes and ears
receiving and perceiving
subtle nuances to navigate
uncharted territories

What I know about intuition is that, above all, it makes illogical leaps of faith worthwhile.

janky is

: disheveled, run-down, and inconsistently reliable

Janky's ginger stubble is becoming slightly gray. He often forgets to eat, then stares off into space and doesn't pretend to understand what you're saying. He can hear you; but, no matter how hard he tries to concentrate, he just can't think.

It's probably because he's hungry.

When Janky turned 65, he started wearing a fanny pack around his waist and filled it with trail mix. Having a handful of almonds, cashews, and cranberries is especially important while doing chores, like repairing his 20-year-old vacuum with duct tape or repositioning his couch.

Janky's couch is propped up on cement cylinders so he can store all of his tools underneath it. If he doesn't distribute his weight evenly on the couch when he sits down, the couch could easily collapse.

Even though his joints are riddled with arthritis, and his eyelids squish together in a wince whenever he stands up, Janky feels encouraged that he can still function, so long as he has that fanny pack snack.

joy is

: a dog's ears flapping, tongue dangling, and teeth grinning
as he sprints forward, drunk on the glory of living like
someone left the gate open

: active, activating, hip-hopping, hop-scotching, and
double-dipping

: a dragonfly resting its kaleidoscope wings under an
infinite summer sky

: blowing wishes into a rainbow of bubbles that disappear
when each one plants a kiss upon a friend's cheek

: a child reminding you that happiness has no requirements
simply by the way they revel in their ice cream

knowing is

: when you close your eyes and see a horizon beyond
what you can see with eyes open

: what makes your chest expand with lightness,
your ribcage feel drizzled with warmth, your hips
tingle like bubbly champagne, and your throat feel
like an upside down waterfall ready to spur forth
inspired words

What I know about knowing is that it lives in the lining of
your guts, the marrow of your bones, the joy of your blood,
and the ears of your heart. And, when you get very still, you
might feel an unquestionable vibrato deep within your core
that makes you know what you know.

lament is

: the volatile entrance
of a memory
that causes convulsions
of sorrow

: the undue struggle
of wishing things to be different
than they are

: an unredeeming meltdown
sustained by believing
your suffering is who you are

What I know about lament is that, once pain is faced,
liberation follows.

What I know about lament is that embracing joy builds
ferocious immunity in the face of injustice.

listening is

: the holy grail of connection

: the frequency, tone, cadence, and warmth of a vibration caressing your heart

: medicine that lets the speaker hear themselves as their wisdom tumbles out

: the honor of witnessing someone exactly as they are

What I know about listening is that it's like fingers reading braille. When you listen not only with your ears, but with all of your senses, you can feel the sediment of sentiments settling in unlit landscapes.

More about listening...

Listening loves to lie down in open fields and revel in the many sounds of the invisible world—sounds that most people tend to miss.

She digests the steadfast, whispered counsel of the trees assuring her she doesn't need to be everyone's audience. She hears the bright fuchsia bougainvillea telling their tales about last night's fiestas, which always reminds her to celebrate more.

Listening is enraptured by the sound of the air wherever she is.

Sometimes the air sounds like a wiry, tinny tightrope ready to snap. Sometimes the air sounds like a warm Gregorian chant soothing her sorrow. Sometimes the air sounds like a leprechaun squealing with delight. Sometimes the air sounds like a harp with a thousand strings offering a dose of respite.

Listening is often misunderstood as not having a lot to say. The truth is she is always combing the landscape of what she hears and feels and is selective in speaking the most important thing that she's gathered. Her greatest gift is to identify what rings as most powerful, true, and important.

One of Listening's favorite activities is to listen to her lover's eyes. The last time she listened to his eyes, she heard a warm bass beat that made her feel like she could swim in stardust. She also loves to listen to the softer language of his fingertips trickling over her back, whispering all the codes that undo the stitches of holding herself together.

a longing is

: like wildfire
devouring
the underbrush of
the psyche
making way for
a clearing
where sunlight
can kiss the seeds
of the heart
and offer it
direction
when it's time
to grow

love is

: a million and one reasons to be together

: a million and one reasons to be apart

: deep connection while laughing, crying, or saying nothing at all

: a warmth that disarms obligations and expectations, while ushering you into a limitless arena of being yourself

: a vehicle that requires no destination

: being the light that you are

What I know about love is that it's an ocean where you can be yourself, lose yourself, and find yourself.

What I know about love is that, when you offer it without conditions, you begin to learn the conditions you require to love yourself.

memory is

: a quiet squatter in a
tiny closet of a stiff muscle,
who never had a chance to cry

: the signature of sentiment
held in chambers of the heart
with 24/7 visiting hours

: a pulse in the bloodline that
whispers what was missing

: a magnifying glass for lessons
that will never be forgotten

: a viewfinder with sweet reminders of summer rain,
freshly-picked strawberries, and dewy grass

: the sticky, sweet scent of raisins at recess

What I know about memory is that it kisses the present with
a portal to the past so we can flourish in every season with
seasoned wisdom.

mercy is

: unexpected grace

Mercy is elegant, sleek, and slender. She wears the scent of fresh rain after a drought and her pheromones smell like gratitude.

Mercy is the most tender embrace you never knew was coming. She is the surprising outlier who says, "I see you," then endows you with ease so you can rise beyond the way the world works.

Mercy doesn't respond to commands, demands, or grocery lists. She moves toward those who surrender control and those who harness their will to soar beyond circumstances. And, for those who have traded judgment for humility, Mercy performs the miracle of turning victimhood into triumph.

money is

: the same vehicle that drives surviving and thriving;
the only difference is the driver—scarcity or abundance

: a beer bottle found in a ditch—one person's careless night
is another person's daily treasure

: a worthy companion who reflects the most compelling and
useful use of energy

When Money is on his game, he wears thick black-rimmed glasses, a bespoke purple blazer, an embroidered silk vest, tailored slacks, and black patent shoes. Money dances with jazz hands on command. He does all sorts of party tricks, like curling his tongue; he believes making someone laugh is always worth it. Money delights in giving personalized gifts— not because he thinks of himself as generous, simply because he revels in seeing others enjoy themselves.

However, sometimes, Money can become distracted when he tries to console his next-door neighbors: Sad, who is unfulfilled, and Anxious, who feels like she's not enough. Money is apt to take Sad to an all-inclusive resort serving unlimited piña coladas, when really, Sad just needs a warm hug.

On the other hand, Anxious has learned that while Money is a blast to play around with, he serves as her greatest mentor when he offers reality checks. Money has a way of calling off the bet and revealing all the ways others under-value their value.

normal is

: a myth

order is

: the feng shui that makes your belly relax, your chest breathe
with relief, and your backbone melt into the couch

: honoring those who contributed to your growth
and development, whether through hard-won lessons
or blessings

: acknowledging that your life's chronology has brought you
to this one momentous moment

passion is

: the faucet of your life force that surges with hard no's
and wild yes's

: the fuel that burns through complacency, ignites desire,
and sets creativity ablaze

: rooted in the right to be alive

What I know about passion is that, when it is mixed with
anger, it changes its name to righteousness and can become
more destructive than creative.

What I know about passion is that, when it co-exists with
compassion, it releases the fight against what's wrong and
allows for embodiment of what's right.

patience is

: a warm well
in the basin of
the belly that
melts all urgency

: an invisible
guest who
brings a dish
of peace
to the table

: a mirror that offers
a drama-free
reflection
of the facts

: grace that unlatches
the need to push
so that you can
feel the pull

: the gardener
who plants timelines
fertilizes the soil
with faith
and watches life
grow in its own
timeless time

: spaciousness
that nurtures
seedlings with lasting
resilience

permission is

What I know about permission is that, with a single exhale, it has the power to shatter the shackles of self-sabotage, self-doubt, self-scrutiny, self-berating, and self-despair.

pleasure is

: a reclamation of your birthright for bliss

: a blueprint for creating heaven on earth

: a resource that doesn't need to be earned or purchased

: the glory that you are expressed through your skin

: the brushstroke of a breeze, a bite of briny sushi,
and the sound of a loved one's belly laugh

: medicine for depression

What I know about pleasure is that savoring it can turn
well-rehearsed narratives into unscripted stories.

poetry is

: a rainbow of nuances between your primary frames
of reference

: a melody that turns the mundane into a miracle

: the rhythm of beauty, the tenor of wonder, and
the tingle of purity

: the art of giving voice to who we are and
who we're becoming

: a chrysalis that nurtures your insides before fluttering into
the hearts of others

: a pilgrimage to loving oneself

Poetry braids peacock feathers into their long, silver hair as
their eyes flicker with mischief and brilliant madness. You
may see Poetry staring into the ethers, searching for just the
right word—one that has been left undefined in the dictionary, yet unlocks the language of their heart.

power is

: clarity bolstering free will and choice

: seeing the humanity in others and the humility in yourself

: bringing parts of yourself that have been separated
back together

: being an ambassador for your needs, desires,
and limitations

: knowing silence can be louder than words when
you've said all you have to say

What I know about power is that pointing a finger at those
who overpower can be a distraction from seeing the ways we
can empower ourselves.

prayer is

: a golden ticket beyond our learned algorithm for reality

: reaching for the reservoir of invisible ears, eyes, and hands
that hold regard for our heart's desires and discontented cries

: a curiosity about the unopened boxes that beckon our reach
in a warehouse of possibilities

What I know about prayer is that it reaches for love beyond
fear, wisdom beyond knowledge, healing beyond pain,
connection beyond separation, joy beyond despair, fulfillment
beyond lack, and possibilities beyond any state of affairs.

What I know about prayer is that it doesn't need a religion,
a vision, a schedule, a how-to manual, or a belief system. All
prayer needs is the honest voice of your heartbeat and the
ears of your soul.

presence is

: naked of expectations

: the most generous gift you can give

Presence glides like a bride walking to the altar of her commitments. She's attentive to every step, infused with an understanding of what she's walking away from and what she's moving toward. Presence is always aware of all people and all things, all at once, just as they are.

purpose is

: deciding to get out of bed every morning

: the intersection between doing and being

Purpose always makes people smile when they catch a glimpse of his colorful socks beneath his khaki pants. He wears pink socks when he wants to feel precious, and lime green socks when he wants to feel focused. Purpose is always accumulating data points about what lights him up and what inspires his growth.

People often associate Purpose with what he does for a living or the ways he chooses to be of service to others. But, what people often dismiss about Purpose is that 80% of his character consists of *how he is being* while he's doing what he's doing.

a quandary is

: when you simply don't know
whether to stay or to go
to do this or that
choose a lizard or a cat
wear a crown or a hat
go for the tit or the tat
be boisterous or flat
be a doctor or an acrobat

: a seemingly impossible decision
riddled with doubt and complexities

An example of a *quandary* used in a sentence, followed by a
short story:

Adele's *quandary* was whether to vacuum up the spider
with an extra-long extension wand or to face her arachnophobia by getting close enough to squish its rotund body
with a Kleenex between her middle finger and thumb.

The risk with vacuuming up the resilient arachnid was that it
could crawl out of the vacuum later, and then dangle from the
ceiling as she slept. Nothing would stop the tiny terror from
spindling its legs through her hair and laying its eggs in her
thick locks.

On the other hand, if Adele risked facing her fear of spiders and crushed the spinster, she'd have to deal with the *quandary* of going against her belief of not harming any living creatures.

Adele considered how she could uphold being a good human by eradicating her harmless intruder without inflicting harm. She pondered fetching a Tupperware container and a piece of paper to trap and then airlift the able-bodied insect to the nearest outdoor area.

However, this plan presented another *quandary*. If Adele could overcome her fear just enough to capture the spider, she would then need to turn over the Tupperware container, remove the flimsy piece of paper, and launch the spider back into the garden with a quick flick of her wrists. Yet, if she didn't flick her wrists quickly enough, the spider could easily escape from its temporary correctional facility and jump up onto her head where, once again, it would nestle into her hair for a thread-spinning marathon.

Adele decided she could not transport the eight-legged threat while it was still living, as there was too much risk of potential mishaps. Adele stared down the bulbous-bodied beast while replaying the worst- and best-case scenarios over and over again in her mind.

You see, the largest part of the *quandary*—even aside from her arachnophobia and her belief system—was her rigorous imagination. Sometimes tiny fears that make no sense whatsoever are the biggest *quandaries* of all.

to receive is

: vulnerable

sacred is

: being devoted to regarding each moment as precious,
rich, and potent

Sacred loves to write letters to her pen pals. She revels in
the ink flowing from her fountain pen as the page absorbs
the curves and shapes of her sentiments. Sacred seals her
scriptures with hot wax and a stamp with her name on it.

Sacred's best-kept secret is that she lives in the mundane.
Sacred loves to spend time with her best friend, Reverence,
because Reverence knows that pulling weeds and planting
roses are equally as precious. Sacred's favorite thing to do with
Reverence is to contemplate all the reasons why staring at
the cosmos makes them feel safe.

self-love is

: Earl Grey tea with frothy milk and honey—awakening, soft, and sweet

: the scent of jasmine—impenetrable, even alongside the stench of a sidewalk baked in rubbish

: enveloping oneself in radical honesty

: knowing that suffering is not a prerequisite for growth

: being wholeheartedly hugged by you—the only one who will be alongside you for life

More about self-love...

: self-love feels like
a goodnight kiss that's
slow to part

: self-love feels like
fireflies glowing with
luminous invitations

: self-love feels like
a glistening lake,
forever reflecting the light of
a thousand summers

: self-love feels like
home

sensitivity is

: a baby's cheeks—soft, innocent, and receptive

: a dog resting its muzzle on your lap when you need
a good cry

: a child telling their parent, "It's going to be okay"

: a cat's ears, pointed to the heavens like pyramids, sensing
the atmosphere before they deem it safe to slink toward you

Sensitivity likes to be naked so her bare skin can sense all the
things she loves, like the sun, the breeze, and the balmy air.
Since Sensitivity listens to her body, she never goes outside
if it's too hot, too cold, or too windy.

Sensitivity has learned that when someone tells her she is
being "too sensitive," they're most likely numb to their own
senses.

Sensitivity doesn't take it personally when others tell her
she's being weak because she was deeply loved by her
grandparents.

Sensitivity's Latin grandmother, Sensus, had the superpower to "feel and perceive." So Sensitivity understands that her gift of feeling heightened physical and emotional sensation is not an impediment; rather, it's her best asset for perceiving important information within the world around her. Sensitivity doesn't shy away from offering the world more precise responses to emotional, intellectual, and political affairs.

Sensitivity's Latin grandfather, Sensitivus, was known for his role of being "capable of sensation." Sensitivus gave others— especially men who were taught not to cry—the permission to feel and express their hurt. He taught two-hour lectures on the repercussions of when pain is stored, stewed, and accidentally expressed as anger.

When Sensitivus encouraged others to focus on sensation, they were able to stay more present and, over time, they became free from the horrors that had previously numbed them from the capacity to feel. His syllabus included his own published studies, somatic exercises, and a list of referrals for therapists.

Thanks to her grandparents' example, Sensitivity spends her time refining her gifts for the benefit of others.

Sometimes, Sensitivity will ask a friend to slow down when they speak. When her friends speak slowly, it allows Sensitivity to connect with their heart instead of their nervous chatter. Almost always, when Sensitivity makes these requests, the other person is grateful. They admit that once they slow down and choose what's most important to share, they feel more connected with Sensitivity and with others.

Sensitivity's grandparents often whisper in her ears, "We're so proud of you for honoring your gift." When she hears their words, Sensitivity sighs; her whole body melts as she feels their embrace, even though they are no longer here.

sensuality is

: awakening the untold story of your spine on the dance floor

: an ecstatic rhapsody rippling through the skin transposing divinity into humanity, and humanity into divinity

: a translator of fear and excitement

: a snake's belly gliding across wet mud, awake to the vulnerability of its legless life and alert to its stealthy power

When Sensuality says your name, the fertility of her voice tells you she belongs to the earth, and so do you.

Many don't understand why it takes Sensuality so long to speak—it's because she's sensing her entire body alongside her heartbeat before oral impulses reach the hum of her vocal chords.

Sensuality savors every note, octave, cadence, arpeggio, and trill of vanilla soufflé sliding from the tip of her tongue to the edges of her 10,000 taste buds as nuanced pleasure fills her cells and is released with an audible *mmmm*.

Sensuality will make you feel naked when she looks at you. She sees the curve of your shoulders collapsing, the clammy temperature of your fingers spreading, and the drapes of despair hanging in your eyes. When you let your nakedness be seen by her wordless gaze, a scintillating zap of aliveness will scurry up the back of your neck, a fuchsia fever will kiss your cheeks, and your heartbeat will quicken even without touch. You may not even know if you're excited or terrified in her presence; yet, one thing is for sure: when you spend time with Sensuality, there's simply no denying you're alive.

shyness is

: a care-full desire to connect

: being pregnant with impulses while hiccupping
on hesitations

: a magnificent value for privacy, coupled with prudence
for being intrusive

: the quiet wisdom of selecting who you trust with your
precious insides

Shyness has long bangs and extraordinarily long eyelashes. When she blinks, her bangs often get threaded through her lashes, so she'll tilt her head sideways to ensure she can have her eyes on you at all times. Her large brown eyes are full of anticipation, yearning for you to come closer—just as much as she is equally ready to skedaddle away. What most people overlook about shyness is that she's a keen observer. She usually has the wisest reflections of anyone in the room. The key is to lean into her observational finesse and pay attention to her nuanced body language as clues for what makes her feel safe enough to contribute her wisdom.

sovereignty is

: accessing power within
versus powering over

: a jaguar
sitting in the jungle
resting in her
permanent authority
with the right
to be alive—
her power is
her presence

Sovereignty has no interest in running for Office because she knows her only job is to be accountable to herself. Besides, she's far too busy. Sovereignty is focused on being the author of her own story and the ambassador for her pleasure, preferences, desires, and dreams.

Sovereignty has become a master at not judging herself for being different from the community she grew up in, known as The Status Quo.

Sovereignty's most important role in self-governance is to evolve what her great-great-great-great-great-great-great-great grand-mother, Gnosis, taught her: "To be true to yourself, you must know yourself. To know yourself, you must be radically honest with yourself."

If Sovereignty is asked a question and she's not clear about her response, she might say something like, "I prefer to wait to give you my answer until I'm 100% clear. Right now, I'm only at 25% clarity." She will not answer just because someone is expecting an answer.

Once, when a near-stranger asked her a very personal question, she considered saying, "I want to be open, but I'm feeling uncomfortable because I'm not familiar enough with you." In the end, she said, "I'm not comfortable answering that question. What else have you got?"

Sovereignty doesn't believe in "including all" for the sake of being a "caring person." She knows that if she's going to be caring for everyone, she needs to include caring for herself. Sometimes this means excluding people who only speak the language of criticism; sometimes it means refraining from smiling like a mechanical doll or exchanging pleasantries when it's not congruent with her feelings inside.

subtlety is

: the moment just before your lips part for a kiss

: each nanosecond between an impulse and an action

What I know about subtlety is that it can be easily missed, yet it is infinitely rich with information.

More about subtlety...

Subtlety is a master pianist who plays one staccato with a tone of urgency and another staccato with a tone of lingering wonder.

Even when Subtlety is playing at full volume, you may need to turn off the white noise of the fridge or the whir of the washing machine just so you can hear, perceive, and sense each note of their music.

to surrender is

: an essential daily supplement

: to release from the pattern of doing and allow the next step to reveal itself

: to let grief erupt knowing it's a measure for how greatly you've loved

: to let all the scaffolding constructed around security come tumbling down

: to realize friendship with the unknown is in reach

: trusting the matrix of life has your back

: to let bliss bring you to the edge of the cliff where a gushing waterfall carries you into surprising thrills

What I know about surrender is that, even when you think you've let go of control, you can still find yourself holding your breath.

What I know about surrender is that it makes your heart softer, your eyes more forgiving, and your smile more sincere.

truth is

: a healing bomb and a healing balm

: a reprieve, a respite, a resonance, and a resolution

: a stake in the ground that strengthens your spine and tows
your bottom line

: a laser that cuts through gray areas, dark nights,
smoke and mirrors, and dust swept under the carpet

: the minister of clarity and the administrator of freedom

What I know about truth is that it'll make you see what you
couldn't see before.

What I know about truth is that, once you give voice to the
griefs, the gouges, the punctures, the ruptures, and the bruises in the company of trusted ears, it will begin to liberate
compassion.

What I know about truth is that, when you embrace it wholeheartedly, it will usher you into the next best version of
yourself.

uncertainty is

: a bloated question mark
floating like a swollen cloud
ready to condense into crystalized
form and find its place on earth

: a viewfinder flickering
back and forth
between a
factless future
and a postulated
present

: lips puckered up
with the possibility
for something
new

a want is

: a close cousin to a whim; it's fleeting in the face of survival

: unlike a need—which is founded on your well-being and fulfillment

: a fixation that can lead to manipulation

: founded on lack and deficiency

What I know about a want is that, unlike desire—which speaks the language of the heart—a want speaks the language of the mind.

What I know about a want is that, unlike a longing—which is your soul tugging you toward the blueprint of your destiny—a want will often lead you toward detours and distractions.

What I know about a want is that *savoring what you have* makes all wants wash away.

wild is

: untethered, unfettered, and free

: calling back the dominion of yourself and
choosing yourself over being chosen

: an urge the surges through your spine, stirs up
your circuitry, and dares you to move toward mystery
and mastery

: knowing you are your own birthstone, touchstone,
milestone, and headstone; you're the one who claims
your right to be you—where you came from, where
you're going, and how you'll exit

: knowing you are your own benchmark, checkmark, and
hallmark; you're the one who ingratiates your growth,
pinpoints your turning points, and certifies your progression
and expression

: non-negotiable

What I know about wild is that there are as many reasons to
be wild as there are hours of daylight and darkness. Wild can
be exposed, but it doesn't need to be seen for it to exist.

More about wild...

Wild tastes like coffee beans—rich, raw, untreated, and undressed.

Wild sounds like cicadas at twilight—hypnotizing you with their rapturous serenades.

Wild smells like tobacco—an unbridled potency that can penetrate your mind with clarity.

Wild feels like a blustering wind—an uncompromising force of nature that extinguishes tiny worries.

xenial is

: to welcome strangers as future friends

: spelled X-E-N-I-A-L; an excellent word for
a triumphant game of Scrabble

: not to be confused with *xennial*, the micro-generation
of people on the cusp of the Generation X and Millennial
demographics

Example of *xenial* used in a sentence:

What the guests found most *xenial* about their host was the
warmth in her eyes that made them feel loved for no reason
at all.

yes is

: a powerful word when you're in agreement with yourself

yesterday is

: permission to begin again

: irrelevant when you don't believe in measuring time

Yesterday wears a burlap dress and likes to aimlessly roll around in dust and tumbleweeds. She blends in with her surroundings and holds disappointments close to her chest. She'll easily rob you from the present if you dwell in her company for too long.

Yesterday likes the feeling of hanging down her head because it feels like she's hanging her hat on a hook after a long day. What Yesterday likes most about herself is that she can remind you of how far you've come.

zahir is

: when you are captivated by something or someone
that calls you to move beyond yourself

What I know about zahir is that, in Arabic, it means visible,
present, and incapable of going unnoticed.

More about zahir...

When you see Zahir, you'll usually feel spellbound that
such a human exists. His lips are plump and always slightly
parted, as though he's about to inhale relief. Zahir wears
mother-of-pearl anklets, white silk gowns, and gold rings
on all his fingers and toes. Zahir has seven white peacocks
and doesn't believe in Mondays or Tuesdays. When Zahir
goes to bed at night, he powders his sheets with rose-scented
baby powder so that he can wake up feeling rosy.

zany is

: a requirement for the well-being of all human beings

: a bestie who sticks licorice up her nose just because

Zany has three cousins: Zippy, Zesty, and Zealous. What Zany and his cousins all have in common is their unbridled enthusiasm for themselves and each other. They have tea while wearing jewel-colored top hats embellished with ribbons of royal blues, emerald greens, and hot pinks. With tea cups in hand and pinkies in the air, they slurp their tea loudly, arch their eyebrows dramatically, and practice their British accents just because it makes them feel fancy.

Serious sermons make Zany and his cousins giggle. At last, when his stepmother Zealot stopped insisting that he listen to her sermons, Zany cut loose, bought himself a rainbow-colored tutu, and joined a local Bingo tournament.

The Author's Deeper "Why"

As much as it is a necessity for me to breathe and dance, *I write to bring my insides to the outside.*

Learning various forms of dance, whether it's tango, pole-dancing, or heels dancing, has allowed me access to a greater repertoire of expression of myself—the same way learning languages has offered a wider possibility of expression through words that I search for and fail to find in English.

Whether I'm learning how to do a head-whip, flicking my hair so it cascades upwards instead of landing in my face, or whether I'm learning how to circle the tip of my toe behind me and thrust my leg around my tango partner, learning new dance moves frees my essence to be expressed through a greater vocabulary of movement.

I'm offering this book to you as a choreographed dance of renewed meaning. Perhaps some of these poetic definitions make connections you have not yet thought of; perhaps some of the words will inspire you to write your own version of definitions.

Overall, my hope is that this collection of re-defining everyday words offers a new perspective as you embrace the permission to stretch the limbs of your mind into new motions. I'm deeply honored you've joined me in attempting to define the undefined, gleaning deeper meaning from our lived experiences, as we bring our precious insides to the outside world, together.

Love,
Rhiah

Appendix

Flowers Featured in Life's Poetic Glossary

Acknowledgements

Infinite thanks...

To my editor, Alexa Johansen, Ph.D., for her rapturous encouragement and for being my trusted poetic confidant and creative sounding board for all stages of design, writing, editing, and publishing.

To my graphic designer, Zeno Zokalj, who brought to life my vision for X-ray images of flowers that mirror humanity, all while applying his own sensibility for emotion to enhance and amplify each poetic definition.

To my trusted first readers, Eli Husserl, Derrick Engoy, Kashmir Birk, Cindy Kennedy, Kim Shirley, Sara Alvarado, and Charlie Jones, who generously reflected on the nuances of my expression, and articulated the purpose of this book far beyond what I could muster.

Krista Kujat, affectionately known as Rhiah by her close friends, was born and raised in Calgary, Canada. She has pole-danced in New York, salsa-ed in Cuba, and tango-ed in Argentina. She's also been known to line dance in saloons, thanks to her early immersion at The Calgary Stampede. Rhiah currently dances her way through Los Angeles studios in four-inch heels and is rigorously working her way up to doing the splits.

Rhiah's fifth-generation Canadian mother and German immigrant father taught her how to clean toilet hinges with Q-tips, color passionately inside the lines, and live outside the box (she grew up with gold shag carpet on the walls). She has a wild appreciation for dreaming beyond the status quo, all while soaking up life's simple pleasures, including fuzzy socks, belly laughs, and breaking the rules.

Rhiah is a winner of the Soul-Making Keats Literary Award and the Independent Spirit Award for film.

Outside of poetry, dancing, and memoir-writing, you may find Rhiah shopping for lingerie, drinking in the timelessness of smooth jazz, or soaking up the sun on a hike. She deeply values the simple act of putting one foot in front of the other.

To follow more of Krista Kujat, you can find her on Instagram at @rhiahkujat.

Krista Kujat is known for her curricula including The Passion Guide, The Sacred Sexy Course, and Principles of Love. Kujat's approach to education and empowerment is focused on liberating oneself from inherited patterns. Her work spans from mentoring others through healing and relational dynamics within family systems, as well as supporting women in cultivating their connection to their sensuality. She leverages inquiry work, intuitive practices, and body-oriented wisdom for lasting inner change. Kujat's future books and curricula are focused on fostering harmonious relating, sovereign sensuality, and sacred intimacy at a global level.

Made in the USA
Monee, IL
22 December 2024

72345876R00119